MW00903919

Confidence

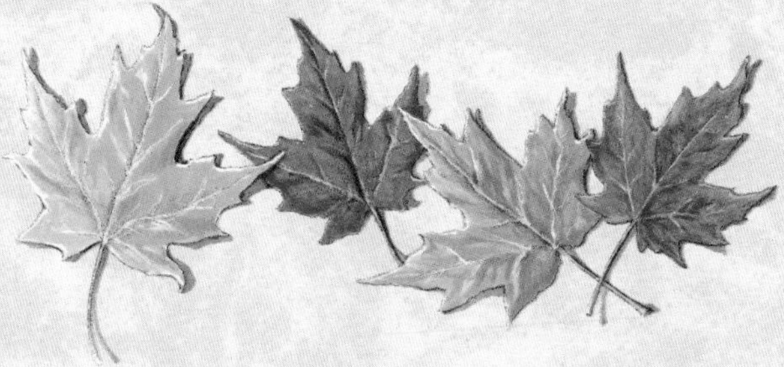

Published by The C.R. Gibson Company
Knight Street, Norwalk, Connecticut
Printed in the United States of America

ISBN 0-8378-2045-6
GB682

Confidence

·Hazelden Encouragements·

Illustrated by
Jody Bishel and Daniel Buckley

The C.R. Gibson Company
Norwalk, Connecticut 06856

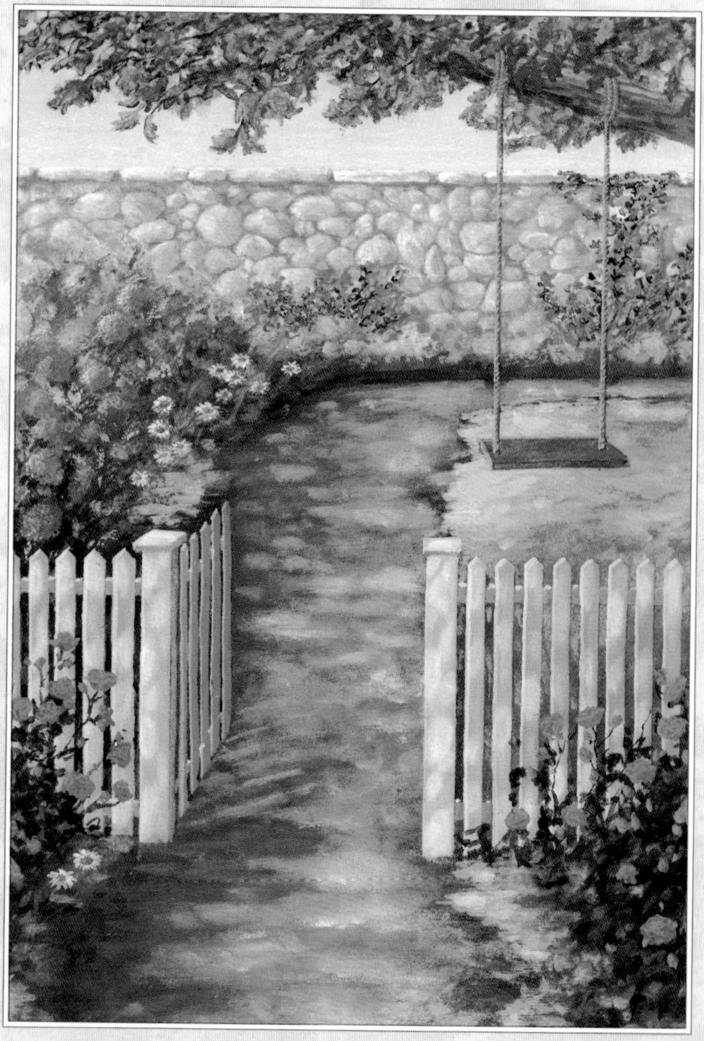

The Gift of Myself

What a great gift we've been given—
ourselves. To listen to ourselves, to trust
instinct and intuition, is to pay tribute to that
gift...What do I need to do to take care of
myself?...What am I being led to do?...What do
I know? Listen, and we will know. Listen to
the voice within.

Melody Beattie

We have been given everything we need
to find our own answers. Although today
may have been filled with questions, we can
remember now that we have all the tools
we need.

Self-confidence, without self-reliance, is as useless as a cooking recipe without food. Self-confidence sees the possibilities of the individual; self-reliance realizes them. Self-confidence sees the angel in the unhewn block of marble; self-reliance carves it out for himself.

William George Jordan

*No one can really pull you up very high—
you lose your grip on the rope.
But on your own two feet
you can climb mountains.*

Louis Brandeis

To walk against the wind once in a while is healthy. We don't always have to follow the crowd if we don't believe the crowd is right. We can be like a lion once in a while: a leader, unafraid to travel alone or to guide others. We can let out a mighty roar that will set us apart from the din of the crowd. We don't have to be sheep all the time, only when we want to be.

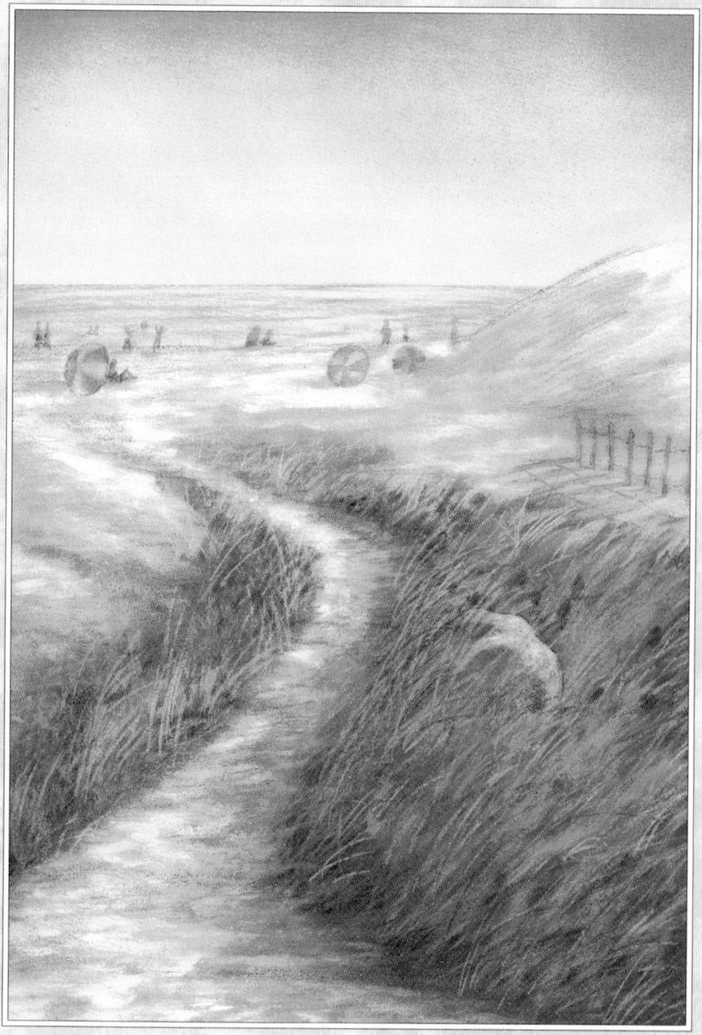

My Feelings

Today I will feel. I will feel wind and water, earth and sun. I will feel rain, the taste of it, the soft sting of its coolness. I will feel the familiar touch of my shirt against my skin, my hair across my face in the wind.

Today I will feel love like a candle on a birthday cake that never goes out, no matter how much you blow on it. I will feel joy and sorrow, pain and pleasure. Today I will feel. I will feel like a human being, unique as a snowflake, common as grass.

The real voyage of discovery consists not in seeking new landscapes but in having new eyes.

Marcel Proust

When we talk about feelings, we often focus on the troublesome trio—pain, fear, and anger. But there are other feelings available in the emotional realm—happiness, joy, peace, contentment, love, closeness, excitement.

It's okay to feel good. We don't have to analyze, judge, or justify. We don't have to bring ourselves down, or let others bring us down, by injecting negativity.

We can let ourselves feel good.

Melody Beattie

Every year businesses go through their files, throwing out old information and papers, and reorganizing remaining files. We can do some cleaning of the message files we keep in our heads.

Stored inside us are messages that no longer hold true. "You're a bad person." "You shouldn't show your feelings." "If you cry, you're not a man." "You'll never amount to anything." "Nobody loves you." We can toss out those old messages. We have learned things are not the way those messages claim they are.

We can start new message files: "I'm a nice person," "Crying is a good way to express my feelings." "It's important for me to show how I feel." "I'm doing wonderful things for myself." "People love me." There's no need to hold onto old files when we have wonderful new ones.

I am ashamed of these tears. And yet
at the extreme of my misfortune
I am ashamed not to shed them.

Euripides

Letting down our guard, releasing the tension that keeps us taut, often invites our tears, tears that soften us, melt our resistance, reveal our vulnerability which reminds us that we are only human.

∾

We should not hide from our tears. We can trust their need to be present for someone else as well as ourselves. Tears encourage compassion.

∾

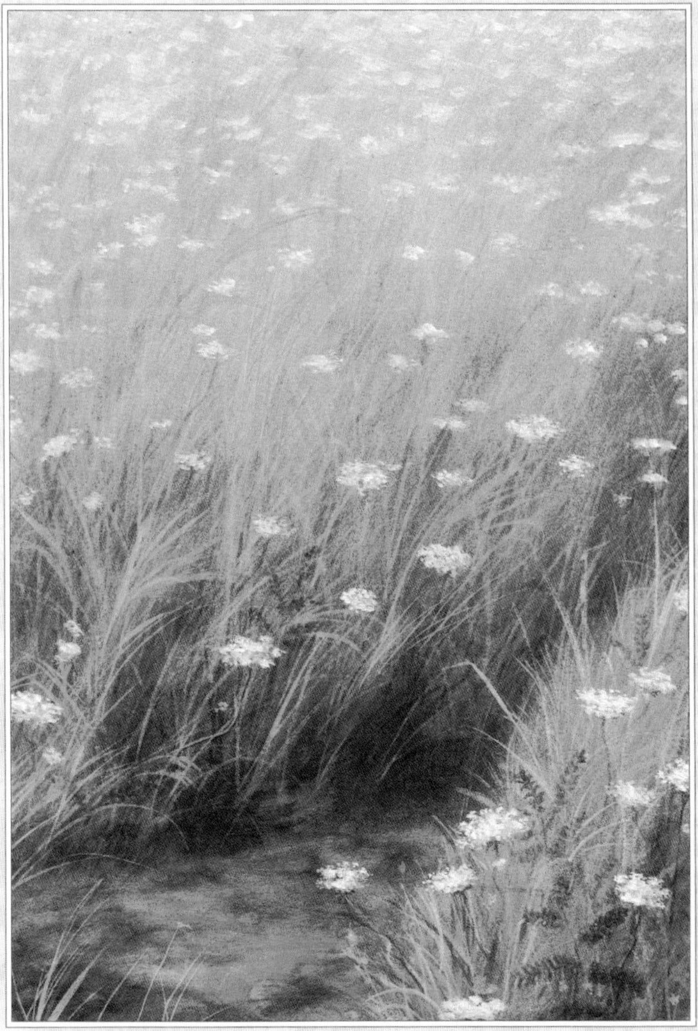

Troubles and Trials

Oh, a trouble's a ton, or a trouble's an ounce, or a trouble is what you make it. And it isn't the fact that you're hurt that counts, but only how you take it.

Edmund Vance Cooke

Once a woman decided to throw a problem exchange party. As guests arrived, they shed all their personal problems and tossed them onto a pile with everyone else's. After all had discussed their own problem for others to hear, the party ended with guests selecting from the problem pile those they wished to carry away. Each person left with the same troubles he or she had brought to the party.

ife is so much better when we aren't drowning in the upsets around us. We don't have to absorb the antics of others or get caught up in the material and mechanical inconveniences. A sure sign of maturity is being able to accept an upset for a few minutes, then let it go.

Many things might be sad,
too bad, and unpleasant —
but the only thing that's the end of the world
is the end of the world.

Melody Beattie

Many times we may believe we should keep our problems to ourselves. Why should we worry others? Or perhaps we don't believe we'll get help and support, only pity and sympathy. Maybe we don't want others to know we have problems.

Everybody has problems, even the people who seem to be all smiles and good cheer. Yet nobody solves problems alone. Many call upon a Higher Power or a close friend. Others use their counselor. Some go to support groups or self-help meetings. All of these people who share their problems will find a solution. It's when we don't use any other sources that our problems become too difficult to handle.

Resolve to be thyself
and know that he who finds himself
loses his misery.

Matthew Arnold

Confidence is that feeling
by which the mind embarks
in great and honourable courses
with a sure hope
and trust in itself.

Cicero

*D*o you ever feel you are wearing a mask? It's a strange, uncomfortable feeling. We mistrust our own face; we don't even know what it looks like, because we put on the mask so young. But sooner or later we must drop it and face our reflection.

Perhaps the mask is silent and behind it we feel like screaming. Perhaps the mask is festive and our own eyes weep.

The mask chafes and confines us, but it gives protection too. We're naked without it; we have nowhere to hide. To summon the courage to drop the mask, we must believe in ourselves enough to trust our naked vulnerability.

We may take courage in knowing that everyone is vulnerable and afraid. By wearing our own faces proudly, we show that it's possible.

*Do not consider anything for your interest
which makes you break your word,
quit your modesty, or inclines you to any
practice which will not bear the light,
or look the world in the face.*

Marcus Antonius

We can let go of our shame
and know instead that it sweetens
the nuggets of the wisdom we can offer to others.
We are alike. We are not without faults.
Our trials help another to smoother sailing.

Live so that you wouldn't be ashamed
to sell the family parrot
to the town gossip.

Will Rogers

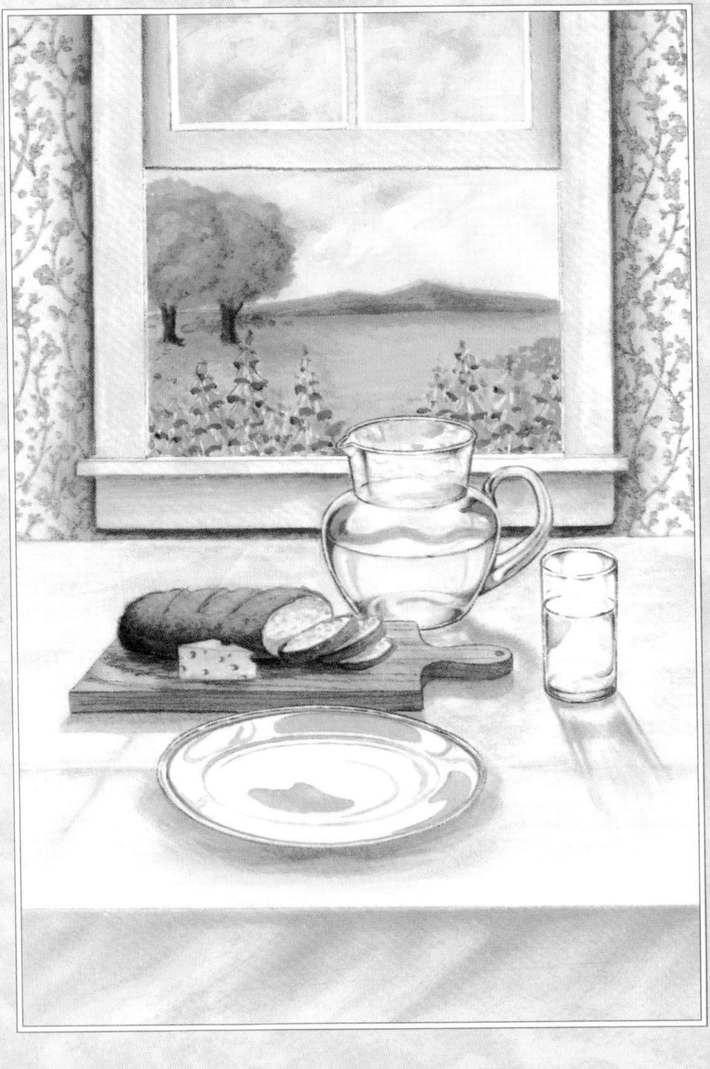

My Needs and Wants

*If there is something
I need from someone,
I will ask first,
before I struggle.*

Melody Beattie

*O*nce there was a woman who loved her husband and children so much that she did everything for them and nothing for herself. She thought taking care of herself was selfish. She never considered taking a vacation when she needed it. She stayed home to take care of her family no matter what it cost her personally. Then she realized how much she resented them because she wasn't taking care of herself. So she began to ask for what she needed. At first, her family didn't like it. Little by little they began to notice that when she was relaxed, their lives were more serene, too.

It wasn't always easy for her to love herself enough to ask for what she needed, but she learned that when she said no to demands she couldn't meet, she felt calm and centered. Best of all, she no longer resented them for asking. When she said yes, she did what they asked with real pleasure.

We can secure other people's approval,
if we do right and try hard;
but our own is worth
a hundred of it...

Mark Twain

We can become all that we want to become.
We can draw the love of others to us
as we more willingly offer love and praise.
We have an opportunity to help one another
as we help ourselves grow in the self-love
that is so necessary to the successful
living of each day.

It's okay to give to others,
but it's okay to keep some for myself, too.

Melody Beattie

Our needs are not great empty pits to be filled any way we can. They are the couplings by which we connect to those we love. Our needs tell us also what others want, and how to enrich their lives—which also enriches ours.

How do we become needed? We have only to look at our own needs and give what we need to others—love, respect, kindness, generosity. When we realize we are needed, we realize we also need others.

The choice of how we want our lives to be is ours. Since we paint a new picture each day, we are always free to change things when they don't please us. What better time than the present?

Rest when you're tired. Take a drink of cold water when you're thirsty. Call a friend when you're lonely. Ask God to help when you feel overwhelmed.

Many of us are afraid the work won't get done if we rest when we're tired. The work will get done; it will be done better than work that emerges from tiredness of soul and spirit.

Melody Beattie

*Confidence will come
with my healthy self-acceptance.*

*I will look forward to challenges
with hope and strength
and know that I am able to meet them.*

The term self-service mostly connotes convenience in shopping. Do we ever truly serve ourselves, in the sense of offering our best to our own benefit? A high quality of self-service is an important part of self-esteem. By taking time for ourselves, treating ourselves gently, we demonstrate our belief that we deserve love.

Quality self-service doesn't only mean caring for our bodies, although that's important. It also means forgiving ourselves, letting mistakes remain in the past, and nourishing our spirits with good thoughts, good words, good deeds. If we're to earn tranquility and joy in life, surely we can learn to serve ourselves with kindness.

Will I be a leader or a follower?
Whichever I choose,
let me believe my choice
is the best for me.

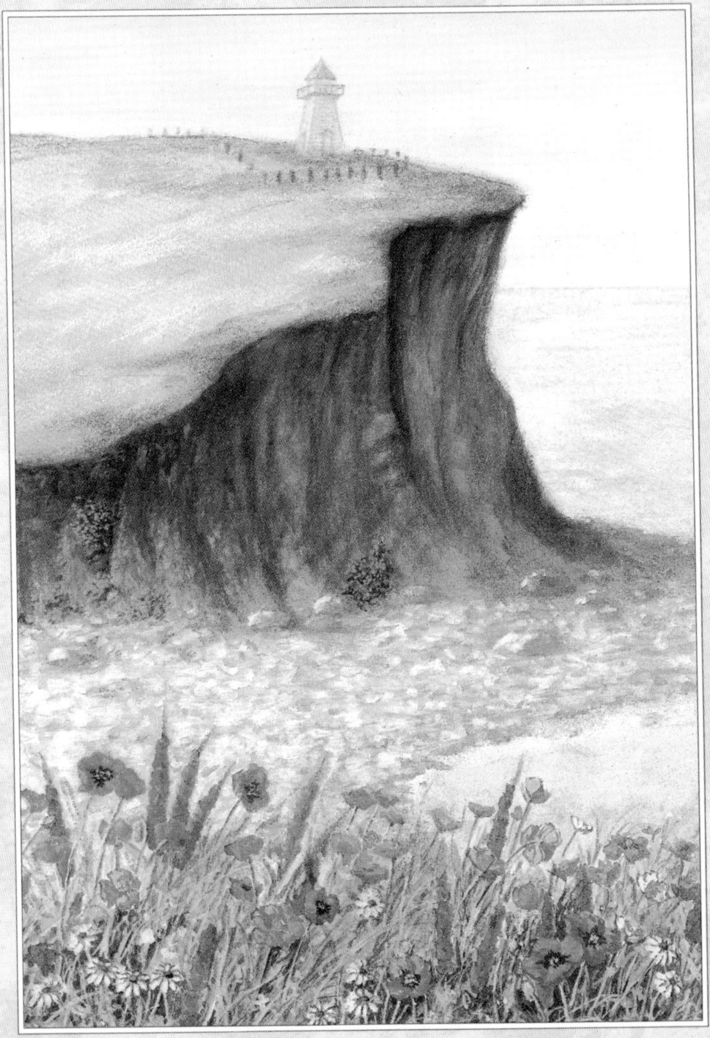

Getting to know our inner geography, our own pattern of needs and fears, is never dangerous. The danger lies in refusing to know. We can't build solid self-confidence on ignorance and mistrust of ourselves. Only by loving ourselves and acknowledging our kinship with needy, fearful humanity can we grow as individuals.

Let us move on, and step out boldly, though it be into the night, and we can scarcely see a way. A Higher Intelligence than the mortal sees the road before us. We do not have to strive for good, but only to go forward and possess it. Good awaits us at every step.

Charles B. Newcomb

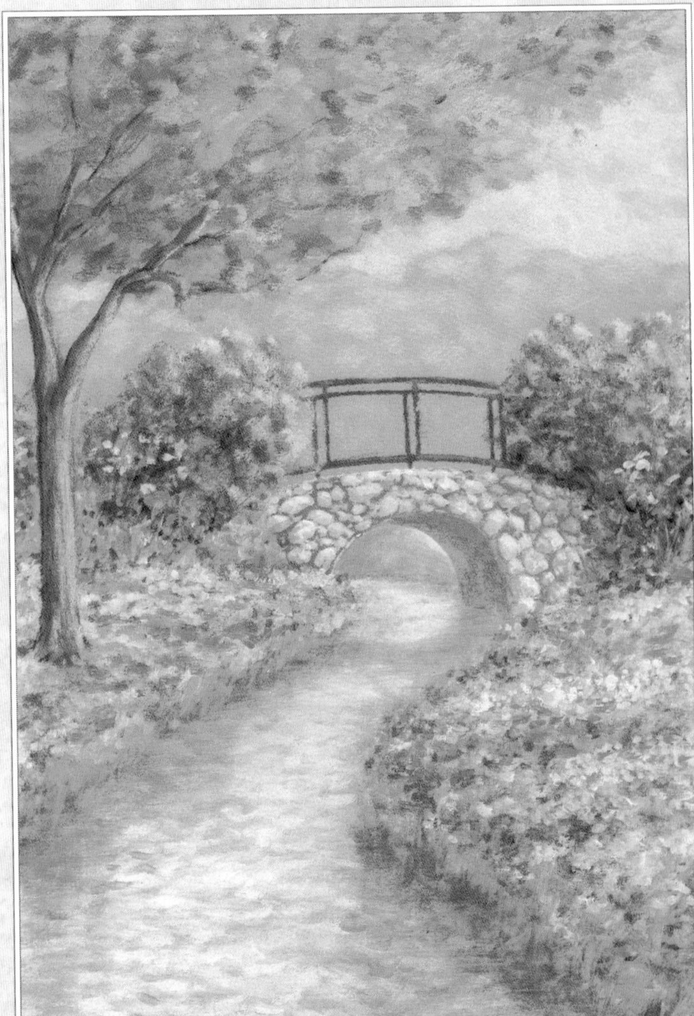

Accepting Me

Liking ourselves doesn't mean
we approve of certain traits or behaviors.
But we can accept them.
We aren't the most perfect companion,
lover, friend or parent.
Neither is anyone else.

Love yourself into health and a good life of
your own.
Love yourself into relationships that work for
you and the other person. Love yourself into
peace, happiness, joy, success and contentment.

Embrace and love all of yourself—past, present, and future. Forgive yourself quickly and as
often as necessary. Encourage yourself. Tell
yourself good things about yourself.

Stop explaining and justifying yourself. When
you make mistakes, let them go. We learn, we
grow, and we learn some more. And through it
all, we love ourselves.

Melody Beattie

*We're in charge of the efforts,
not the results.*

*We are never guaranteed
success by others' standards.
However, if we do our best
according to our standards
we'll be successful.*

We have many chances for growth,
for kindness to others,
and for developing
confidence in ourselves.

You don't have to handle it alone.

Personal freedom means choosing our own behavior; it means acting rather than reacting. It also means allowing ourselves the full adventure of living, of meeting each moment wholly, of responding in a pure, spontaneous, personally honest manner. Only then can we give to life what is ours to give.

Each of us has a unique part to play in the drama of life. And we need to rely on our Higher Power for our cues, not on those whose approval we think we need. When we turn within for guidance, all the approval we could hope for will be ours.

$\mathcal{N}$urtured, nourished people,
who love themselves and care for themselves,
are the delight of the Universe.
They are well-timed, efficient, and Divinely led.

Melody Beattie

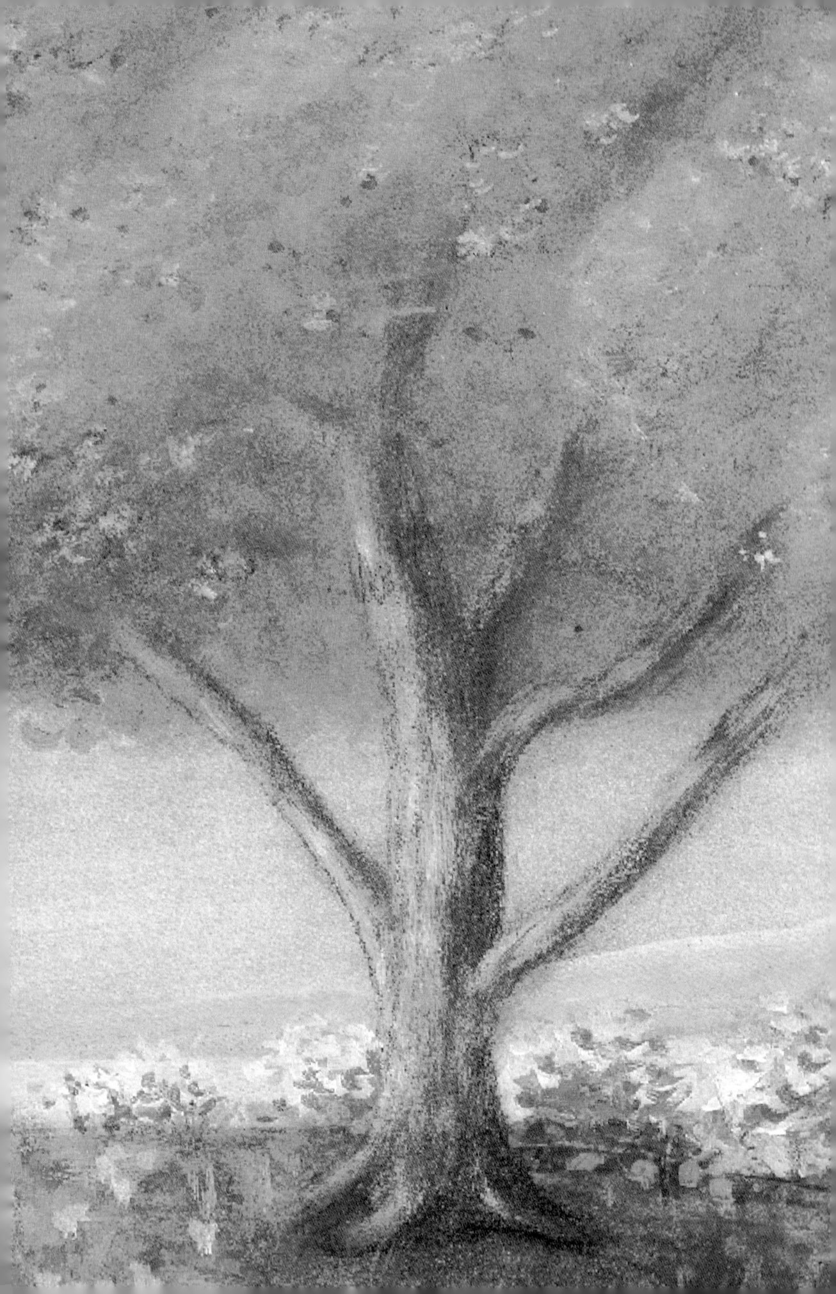

Each of us blooms in our own time,
with our own color and fragrance.
Every one of us is a
special and important blossom,
and we are all part of the tree of life.

Colophon

Compiled and edited by Stephanie C. Oda
Designed by Aurora Campanella Lyman
Calligraphed by Martin Holloway
Type set in Kunstler Script, Bodoni Book Italic